T0071674

SCHIRMER'S LIBRARY
OF MUSICAL CLASSICS

Vol. 1236

Edouard Lalo

Op. 21

Symphonie Espagnole

For Violin and Piano

Edited by

LEOPOLD LICHTENBERG

G. SCHIRMER, Inc.

DISTRIBUTED BY

HAL•LEONARD®
CORPORATION
7777 W BLUEMOUND RD P O BOX 13819 MILWAUKEE, WI 53213

Copyright, 1915, by G. Schirmer, Inc.

Printed in the U. S. A.

2

Edited by Leopold Lichtenberg

Dedicated to Pablo Sarasate

Symphonie Espagnole

No. 1

Édouard Lalo. Op. 21

Copyright, 1915, by G. Schirmer, Inc.
Printed in the U.S.A.

No. 2

Scherzando

Tempo I°

No. 3
Intermezzo

Allegretto non troppo (♩=76)

Violin

SCHIRMER'S LIBRARY
OF MUSICAL CLASSICS

Vol. 1236

EDOUARD LALO

Op. 21

Symphonie Espagnole

For Violin and Piano

Edited by

LEOPOLD LICHTENBERG

G. SCHIRMER, *Inc.*

DISTRIBUTED BY

HAL•LEONARD®
CORPORATION

7777 W BLUEMOUND RD P O BOX 13819 MILWAUKEE, WI 53213

Copyright, 1915, by G. Schirmer, Inc.

Printed in the U. S. A.

Symphonie Espagnole

Nº 1

Violin

Edited by Leopold Lichtenberg

Édouard Lalo. Op. 21

Allegro non troppo (♩ = 84)

Down-bow
Up-bow
String

Printed in the U.S.A.

Copyright, 1915, by G. Schirmer, Inc.

Violin

*) Broad and sustained

Violin

*) Broad and sustained

Violin
№ 2
Scherzando

№ 3

Intermezzo

*) Broad and sustained

Violin

№ 4

Printed in the U.S.A.
Copyright, 1915, by G. Schirmer, Inc.

Violin

Nº 5
Rondo

*) The introduction for Orchestra is **10** measures longer than that for Piano

Violin

No. 4

Printed in the U.S.A.
Copyright, 1915, by G. Schirmer, Inc.

Tempo I°

No. 5
Rondo

Tempo I°